ROYAL COU

Royal Court Theatre presents

# SCENES FROM
# THE BACK OF BEYOND
by **Meredith Oakes**

First performance at the Royal Court Jerwood Theatre Upstairs,
Sloane Square, London on 2 November 2006.

# SCENES FROM THE BACK OF BEYOND

by **Meredith Oakes**

Guy **Luke Bromley**
Helen **Penny Downie**
David **Daniel Lapaine**
Jasmine **Samantha Losey**
Robbo **Tom Sangster**
Bill **Martin Turner**

Director **Ramin Gray**
Designer **Jon Bausor**
Lighting Designer **Johanna Town**
Sound Designer **Emma Laxton**
Assistant Directors **Joe Douglas, Kathryn Ind**
Casting **Amy Ball**
Production Managers **Sue Bird, Paul Handley**
Stage Managers **Nafeesah Butt, Sarah Tryfan**
Work Placements **Gabriel Kirshner, Alison Rich**
Costume Supervisor **Laura Hunt**
Movement **Shona Morris**
Dialect Coach **Joan Washington**
Set built by **Rupert Blakeley**

The Royal Court wish to thank **Annie Castledine** for her valuable contribution to the development of this production.

## THE COMPANY

**Meredith Oakes** (writer)
For the Royal Court: The Editing Process, Faith.
As translator for the Royal Court: Werner Schwab's Holy Mothers (Die Präsidentinnen).
Other theatre includes: The Neighbour (National); Mind the Gap (Hampstead); Man for Hire (Scarborough); Shadowmouth (Crucible Studio).
Other translations include: Schiller's Kabale und Liebe, Strindberg's Miss Julie, Horvath's Italian Night, Bernhard's Elizabeth II, Lenz's The New Menoza.
Radio includes: Glide, Trampoline, The Mind of the Meeting.

**Jon Bausor** (designer)
Theatre includes: The Soldier's Tale (Old Vic); Shrieks of Laughter (Soho); The Great Highway (Gate); Cymbeline (Regent's Park); The Hoxton Story (Red Room); Frankenstein (Derby Playhouse); Bread and Butter (Oxford Stage Company/Tricycle); Carver, Mariana Pineda (Arcola); The Last Waltz Season (OSC/ Dumbfounded); Melody, In The Bag (Traverse); The New Tenant, Interior, The Exception and the Rule, Winners, The Soul of Chien-Nu (Young Vic); Sanctuary, The Tempest (National); The Taming of the Shrew (Thelma Holt/Theatre Royal, Plymouth/tour); Switchback, Possible Worlds (Tron, Glasgow).
Dance includes: Snow White in Black (Phoenix Dance Theatre/Sadler's Wells); Ghosts, Before the Tempest…, Sophie, Stateless, Asyla (Linbury/ROH); Mixtures (Westminster Abbey/English National Ballet); Non Exeunt (George Piper Dances/Sadler's Wells).
Opera includes: The Knot Garden (Klangbogen Festival, Vienna); The Queen of Spades (Edinburgh Festival Theatre); Cosi fan Tutte (Handmade Opera); King Arthur (New Chamber Opera).

**Luke Bromley**
Theatre includes: Annie, Carousel, Barnum (Wimbledon); Singin' in the Rain (Richmond); The Wiz, Annie Get Your Gun, Bugsy Malone (Hampton Hill); Summer Holiday (Leatherhead).
Television includes: The Comedy Lab, Planet Cook, Living It, The Bill, That Mitchell Webb

Look, Torchwood.
Film includes: Between Us, Kodak BAFTA finale, Harry Potter and the Order of the Phoenix.

**Joe Douglas** (assistant director)
For the Royal Court as Directing Placement: Motortown.
As director: Manifest! (YMT:UK); Fantasy Football, One for the Road (BAC); A Christmas Carol, The New World Order, Original (Catholic) Doubt, Face to the Wall (Rose Bruford).
As assistant director: Red Hunter, Amy's Wedding (YMT:UK); Man Equals Man (Rose Bruford); Orvin (Scarborough); Tom's Midnight Garden (Library Theatre, Manchester).

**Penny Downie**
For the Royal Court: Berlin Bertie.
Other theatre includes: Dinner (National/ West End); Henry V, An Enemy of the People, Sleep with Me, Tantalus (National); A Midsummer Night's Dream, Romeo and Juliet, Richard III, Today, Dream Play, The Castle, Crimes in Hot Countries, A Winter's Tale, Macbeth, Art of Success, The Plantagenets, The Merchant of Venice, Zenobia, The Prisoner's Dilemma (RSC); Scenes from a Marriage (Wyndham's); Death and the Maiden (Duke of York's); An Ideal Husband (Haymarket/ Broadway); A Map of the World (Sydney Theatre Co.); Privates on Parade (National Theatre, Western Australia); seasons with Sydney Theatre Co., Tasmanian Theatre Co.
Television includes: New Street Law, Girl in a Café, Byron, Poirot, All About George, Trial and Retribution, It Happens, Falling, Murder in Rome, Sherlock Holmes, Inspector Linley, Spooks, Minder, Campaign, A Taste for Death, Stanley and the Women, Ex, Underbelly, Inspector Morse, Paradise, The Governor, Madson, The Ice House, Survivor – Jungle, A Certain Justice, Lost for Words, Kavanagh QC, Trust, The Cazalets.
Australian television includes: Sullivans, Prisoner Cell Block H, Learned Friends, The Box, Bellbird.
Film includes: House of Mirth, Crime and Punishment, Food of Love, Lionheart, Wetherby, Cross Talk, Around the Bend.
Penny is an Associate Artist for the RSC.

**Ramin Gray** (director)
For the Royal Court: Woman and Scarecrow, Motortown, Way to Heaven, Bear Hug, The Weather, Ladybird, Advice to Iraqi Women, Terrorism, Night Owls, Just a Bloke, Push Up, How I Ate a Dog.
Other theatre includes: The American Pilot (RSC); The Child, The Invisible Woman (Gate); Cat and Mouse (Sheep) (Théâtre National de l'Odéon, Paris/Gate); Autumn and Winter (Man in the Moon); A Message for the Broken-Hearted (Liverpool Playhouse/BAC); At Fifty She Discovered the Sea, Harry's Bag, Pig's Ear, A View from the Bridge (Liverpool Playhouse); The Malcontent (Latchmere).
Ramin is Associate Director of the Royal Court.

**Kathryn Ind** (assistant director)
As director, theatre includes: And All Because, Antigone (BAC); The Pitchfork Disney, Funeral Parlor, Meet the Whitbreads, Who's Afraid of Virginia Woolf?, Fear and Misery in the Third Reich (Rose Bruford); Skryker (Barn Theatre, Sidcup); First Impressions, The Peasant of El Salvador (Edinburgh Fringe Festival).
Film includes: First Date, Dice Man, Mars and Venus.
As assistant director, theatre includes: Playboy of the Western World (tour); Clever Dick (Hampstead); Caucasian Chalk Circle (Rose Bruford); Glue, The Twits (Citizens, Glasgow); The Seagull (Dundee Rep); Macbeth (Northern Broadsides).

**Daniel Lapaine**
For the Royal Court: Fucking Games.
Other theatre includes: Les Parents Terribles, King Lear (Sydney Theatre Co.); Island (Belvoir Street Theatre); Romeo and Juliet, Richard III, Hamlet (Bell Shakespeare Co.).
Television: The Good Housekeeping Guide, Jane Hall, Golden Hour, Jericho, Death on the Nile, Red Cap, Helen of Troy, I Saw You, Tenth Kingdom.
Film: Collusion, The Abduction Club, Ritual, The Journeyman, Double Jeopardy, Elephant Juice, Brokedown Palace, 54, Say You'll Be Mine, 1999, Dangerous Beauty, Polish Wedding, Lucinda 31, Muriel's Wedding.

**Emma Laxton** (sound designer)
For the Royal Court: Woman and Scarecrow, The World's Biggest Diamond, Incomplete and Random Acts of Kindness, My Name Is Rachel Corrie (also West End/Galway Festival/Edinburgh Festival/Minetta Lane, New York), Bone, The Weather, Bear Hug, Terrorism, Food Chain.
Other theatre includes: Other Hands (Soho); The Unthinkable (Sheffield); My Dad is a Birdman (Young Vic); The Gods Are Not to Blame (Arcola); Late Fragment (Tristan Bates Theatre).
Emma is Sound Deputy at the Royal Court.

**Samantha Losey**
This is Samantha's debut performance.

**Tom Sangster**
Theatre includes: The Vegemite Tales (Riverside Studios/The Venue); Etta Jenks (Weaver Hughes Ensemble); Manon/Sandra (Edinburgh Fringe).
Television includes: Basil Brush Show.
Film includes: Zone 3, The Portal, Treat 'em Mean, The Fan, La Primera Fiesta, The Fab Four, Park Love.

**Johanna Town** (lighting designer)
For the Royal Court: My Name is Rachel Corrie (& West End/Galway Festival/Edinburgh Festival/Minetta Lane, New York), Rainbow Kiss, The Winterling, The Woman Before, Way To Heaven, A Girl in a Car With a Man, Under the Whaleback, The Kitchen, O Go My Man (with Out of Joint), Talking to Terrorists (with Out of Joint), Shopping and Fucking (with Out of Joint/West End), The Steward of Christendom (with Out of Joint/Broadway).
Other theatre includes: Guantanamo (Tricycle/West End/New York); Rose (National/New York); Arabian Nights, Our Lady of Sligo (New York); Little Malcolm and His Struggle Against the Eunuchs (West End/Hampstead); Feelgood, Top Girls, Via Dolorosa, Beautiful Thing (West End); To Kill A Mocking Bird (Birmingham Rep/ tour); The Glassroom (Hampstead); The Overwhelming, The Permanent Way, She Stoops to Conquer (Out of Joint/National); Macbeth (Out of Joint

world tour); In Praise of Love (Chichester); Dead Funny (West Yorkshire Playhouse); All the Ordinary Angels (Royal Exchange); East Coast Chicken Supper (Traverse); Helen of Troy (ATC); How Love is Spelt (Bush); I.D. (Almeida/BBC3); Badnuff (Soho); The Dumb Waiter (Oxford); Popcorn (Liverpool Playhouse).

Jo is Head of Lighting at the Royal Court and has lit over 50 productions.

**Martin Turner**
Theatre includes: Rabbit (Trafalgar Studios); Gaddafi (ENO); A Midsummer Night's Dream (RSC with City of London Sinfonia/RSC with Orchestra Age Enlightenment); Promises Promises (Sheffield Crucible); Silk Stockings (Lost Musicals); A Conversation, Blithe Spirit (Royal Exchange); Pericles (Lyric Hammersmith); Protection (Soho); Dealer's Choice/My Night with Reg (Birmingham Rep); Alice in Wonderland, A Midsummer Night's Dream, Love's Labour's Lost, Gentlemen Prefer Blondes, Troilus & Cressida (Regent's Park); Two Noble Kinsmen, The Tempest, St Augustine's Oak, Comedy of Errors (Globe); Phaedre (BAC); Martin Guerre, Anything Goes (Prince Edward); The Crucible, Private Lives (Salisbury); Amadeus (Northcott); Madness in Valencia (Gate); La Chunga (Old Red Lion); Trumpets and Drums (York); She Stoops to Conquer (Liverpool Everyman); Macbeth, A Midsummer Night's Dream, The Man of Mode, Andromache, Pericles, Vanity Fair (Cheek by Jowl).

Television includes: Judge John Deed, The Somme, Rosemary and Thyme, Doctors, Abolition, Holby City, Cromwell Warts and All, Charles II, Foyle's War, The Knock, Family Affairs, Killer Net, Pie in the Sky, The Bill, Dangerfield, Do The Right Thing, You Me and It, Casualty, Trainer, Queen of Fruit, Poirot, Bergerac, High Street Blues, Rumpole of the Bailey, At the Café Continental, The Bill, The Money Men.

Film includes: Prince William.

## THE ENGLISH STAGE COMPANY AT THE ROYAL COURT

The English Stage Company at the Royal Court opened in 1956 as a subsidised theatre producing new British plays, international plays and some classical revivals.

The first artistic director George Devine aimed to create a writers' theatre, 'a place where the dramatist is acknowledged as the fundamental creative force in the theatre and where the play is more important than the actors, the director, the designer'. The urgent need was to find a contemporary style in which the play, the acting, direction and design are all combined. He believed that 'the battle will be a long one to continue to create the right conditions for writers to work in'.

Devine aimed to discover 'hard-hitting, uncompromising writers whose plays are stimulating, provocative and exciting'. The Royal Court production of John Osborne's Look Back in Anger in May 1956 is now seen as the decisive starting point of modern British drama and the policy created a new generation of British playwrights. The first wave included John Osborne, Arnold Wesker, John Arden, Ann Jellicoe, N F Simpson and Edward Bond. Early seasons included new international plays by Bertolt Brecht, Eugène Ionesco, Samuel Beckett and Jean-Paul Sartre.

The theatre started with the 400-seat proscenium arch Theatre Downstairs, and in 1969 opened a second theatre, the 60-seat studio Theatre Upstairs. Some productions transfer to the West End, such as My Name is Rachel Corrie, Terry Johnson's Hitchcock Blonde, Caryl Churchill's Far Away and Conor McPherson's The Weir. Recent touring productions include Sarah Kane's 4.48 Psychosis (US tour) and Ché Walker's Flesh Wound (Galway Arts Festival). The Royal Court also co-produces plays which transfer to the West End or tour internationally, such as Conor McPherson's Shining City (with Gate Theatre, Dublin), Sebastian Barry's The Steward of Christendom and Mark Ravenhill's Shopping and Fucking (with Out of Joint), Martin McDonagh's The Beauty Queen Of Leenane (with Druid), Ayub Khan Din's East is East (with Tamasha).

Since 1994 the Royal Court's artistic policy has again been vigorously directed to finding and producing a new generation of playwrights. The writers include Joe Penhall, Rebecca Prichard, Michael Wynne, Nick Grosso, Judy Upton, Meredith Oakes, Sarah Kane, Anthony Neilson, Judith Johnson, James Stock, Jez Butterworth, Marina Carr, Phyllis Nagy, Simon Block, Martin

photo: Stephen Cummiiskey

McDonagh, Mark Ravenhill, Ayub Khan Din, Tamantha Hammerschlag, Jess Walters, Ché Walker, Conor McPherson, Simon Stephens, Richard Bean, Roy Williams, Gary Mitchell, Mick Mahoney, Rebecca Gilman, Christopher Shinn, Kia Corthron, David Gieselmann, Marius von Mayenburg, David Eldridge, Leo Butler, Zinnie Harris, Grae Cleugh, Roland Schimmelpfennig, Chloe Moss, DeObia Oparei, Enda Walsh, Vassily Sigarev, the Presnyakov Brothers, Marcos Barbosa, Lucy Prebble, John Donnelly, Clare Pollard, Robin French, Elyzabeth Gregory Wilder, Rob Evans, Laura Wade, Debbie Tucker Green and Simon Farquhar. This expanded programme of new plays has been made possible through the support of A.S.K. Theater Projects and the Skirball Foundation, The Jerwood Charity, the American Friends of the Royal Court Theatre and (in 1994/5 and 1999) the National Theatre Studio.

The refurbished theatre in Sloane Square opened in February 2000, with a policy still inspired by the first artistic director George Devine. The Royal Court is an international theatre for new plays and new playwrights, and the work shapes contemporary drama in Britain and overseas.

The Royal Court's long and successful history of innovation has been built by generations of gifted and imaginative individuals. In 2006, the company celebrates its 50th Anniversary, an important landmark for the performing arts in Britain. For information on the many exciting ways you can help support the theatre, please contact the Development Department on 020 7565 5079.

# AWARDS FOR
# THE ROYAL COURT

Martin McDonagh won the 1996 George Devine Award, the 1996 Writers' Guild Best Fringe Play Award, the 1996 Critics' Circle Award and the 1996 Evening Standard Award for Most Promising Playwright for The Beauty Queen of Leenane. Marina Carr won the 19th Susan Smith Blackburn Prize (1996/7) for Portia Coughlan. Conor McPherson won the 1997 George Devine Award, the 1997 Critics' Circle Award and the 1997 Evening Standard Award for Most Promising Playwright for The Weir. Ayub Khan Din won the 1997 Writers' Guild Awards for Best West End Play and New Writer of the Year and the 1996 John Whiting Award for East is East (co-production with Tamasha).

Martin McDonagh's The Beauty Queen of Leenane (co-production with Druid Theatre Company) won four 1998 Tony Awards including Garry Hynes for Best Director. Eugene Ionesco's The Chairs (co-production with Theatre de Complicite) was nominated for six Tony awards. David Hare won the 1998 Time Out Live Award for Outstanding Achievement and six awards in New York including the Drama League, Drama Desk and New York Critics Circle Award for Via Dolorosa. Sarah Kane won the 1998 Arts Foundation Fellowship in Playwriting. Rebecca Prichard won the 1998 Critics' Circle Award for Most Promising Playwright for Yard Gal (co-production with Clean Break).

Conor McPherson won the 1999 Olivier Award for Best New Play for The Weir. The Royal Court won the 1999 ITI Award for Excellence in International Theatre. Sarah Kane's Cleansed was judged Best Foreign Language Play in 1999 by Theater Heute in Germany. Gary Mitchell won the 1999 Pearson Best Play Award for Trust. Rebecca Gilman was joint winner of the 1999 George Devine Award and won the 1999 Evening Standard Award for Most Promising Playwright for The Glory of Living.

In 1999, the Royal Court won the European theatre prize New Theatrical Realities, presented at Taormina Arte in Sicily, for its efforts in recent years in discovering and producing the work of young British dramatists.

Roy Williams and Gary Mitchell were joint winners of the George Devine Award 2000 for Most Promising Playwright for Lift Off and The Force of Change respectively. At the Barclays Theatre Awards 2000 presented by the TMA, Richard Wilson won the Best Director Award for David Gieselmann's Mr Kolpert and Jeremy Herbert won the Best Designer Award for Sarah Kane's 4.48 Psychosis. Gary Mitchell won the Evening Standard's Charles Wintour Award 2000 for Most Promising Playwright for The Force of Change. Stephen Jeffreys' I Just Stopped by to See the Man won an AT&T: On Stage Award 2000.

David Eldridge's Under the Blue Sky won the Time Out Live Award 2001 for Best New Play in the West End. Leo Butler won the George Devine Award 2001 for Most Promising Playwright for Redundant. Roy Williams won the Evening Standard's Charles Wintour Award 2001 for Most Promising Playwright for Clubland. Grae Cleugh won the 2001 Olivier Award for Most Promising Playwright for Fucking Games.

Richard Bean was joint winner of the George Devine Award 2002 for Most Promising Playwright for Under the Whaleback. Caryl Churchill won the 2002 Evening Standard Award for Best New Play for A Number. Vassily Sigarev won the 2002 Evening Standard Charles Wintour Award for Most Promising Playwright for Plasticine. Ian MacNeil won the 2002 Evening Standard Award for Best Design for A Number and Plasticine. Peter Gill won the 2002 Critics' Circle Award for Best New Play for The York Realist (English Touring Theatre). Ché Walker won the 2003 George Devine Award for Most Promising Playwright for Flesh Wound. Lucy Prebble won the 2003 Critics' Circle Award and the 2004 George Devine Award for Most Promising Playwright, and the TMA Theatre Award 2004 for Best New Play for The Sugar Syndrome.

Richard Bean won the 2005 Critics' Circle Award for Best New Play for Harvest. Laura Wade won the 2005 Critics' Circle Award for Most Promising Playwright and the 2005 Pearson Best Play Award for Breathing Corpses. The 2006 Whatsonstage Theatregoers' Choice Award for Best New Play was won by My Name is Rachel Corrie.

The 2005 Evening Standard Special Award was given to the Royal Court 'for making and changing theatrical history this last half century'.

# ROYAL COURT BOOKSHOP

The Royal Court bookshop offers a range of contemporary plays and publications on the theory and practice of modern drama. The staff specialise in assisting with the selection of audition monologues and scenes. Royal Court playtexts from past and present productions cost £2.

The Bookshop is situated just above the ROYAL COURT CAFE BAR.

**Monday–Friday 3–10pm**

**Saturday 2.30–10pm**

**For information tel: 020 7565 5024**

**or email: bookshop@royalcourttheatre.com**

# PROGRAMME SUPPORTERS

The Royal Court (English Stage Company Ltd) receives its principal funding from Arts Council England, London. It is also supported financially by a wide range of private companies, charitable and public bodies, and earns the remainder of its income from the box office and its own trading activities.

The Genesis Foundation supports the Royal Court's work with International Playwrights.

Archival recordings of the Royal Court's Anniversary year are made possible by Francis Finlay.

The Skirball Foundation funds a Playwrights' Programme at the theatre. The Artistic Director's Chair is supported by a lead grant from The Peter Jay Sharp Foundation, contributing to the activities of the Artistic Director's office. Over the past nine years the BBC has supported the Gerald Chapman Fund for directors.

The Jerwood Charity supports new plays by new playwrights through the Jerwood New Playwrights series.

ARTS COUNCIL ENGLAND

# FOR THE ROYAL COURT

Royal Court Theatre, Sloane Square, London SW1W 8AS
Tel: 020 7565 5050 Fax: 020 7565 5001
info@royalcourttheatre.com
www.royalcourttheatre.com

Artistic Director **Ian Rickson**
Associate Director International **Elyse Dodgson**
Associate Director **Ramin Gray**
Associate Director Casting **Lisa Makin**
Associate Director (50th) **Emily McLaughlin+**
Associate Directors* **James Macdonald,
Max Stafford-Clark, Richard Wilson**
Literary Manager **Graham Whybrow**
Literary Associate **Terry Johnson***
Casting Deputy **Amy Ball**
International Associate **Orla O'Loughlin**
International Administrator **Chris James**
Trainee Director **Lyndsey Turner**
Artistic Assistant **Rebecca Hanna-Grindall**

Production Manager **Paul Handley**
Deputy Production Manager **Sue Bird**
Production Assistant **Sarah Davies**
Head of Lighting **Johanna Town**
Lighting Deputy **Greg Gould**
Lighting Assistants **Nicki Brown, Kelli Marston**
Lighting Board Operator **Stephen Andrews**
Head of Stage **Steven Stickler**
Stage Deputy **Daniel Lockett**
Stage Chargehand **Lee Crimmen**
Head of Sound **Ian Dickinson**
Sound Deputy **Emma Laxton**
Acting Head of Costume **Laura Hunt**
Costume Deputy **Jackie Orton**

YOUNG WRITERS PROGRAMME
Associate Director **Ola Animashawun**
Administrator **Nina Lyndon**
Administrator (Maternity Cover) **Claire Birch**
Outreach Worker **Lucy Dunkerley**
Education Officer **Laura McCluskey***
Writers' Tutor **Leo Butler***

General Manager **Diane Borger**
Administrator **Oliver Rance**
Finance Director **Sarah Preece**
Finance Officer **Rachel Harrison***
Finance Officer **Martin Wheeler**
Finance Manager **Helen Perryer***

Head of Press **Ewan Thomson**
Press Associate **Tamsin Treverton Jones***
Press Assistant **Steve Pidcock**
Press Intern **Amanda Dekker**

Marketing Consultant **Kym Bartlett***
Advertising and Marketing Agency **aka**
Marketing Assistant **Gemma Frayne**
Marketing Intern **Áine Mulkeen**
Sales Manager **David Kantounas**
Deputy Sales Manager **Stuart Grey**
Box Office Sales Assistants **Helen Bennett,
Maria Ferran, Samantha Preston**

Head of Development **Nicky Jones**
Development Manager **Leona Felton**
Trusts and Foundations Manager **Gaby Styles**
Sponsorship Officer **Natalie Moss**
Development Intern **Rebecca Bond**

Theatre Manager **Bobbie Stokes**
Front of House Managers **Nathalie Meghriche,
Lucinda Springett**
Bar and Food Manager **Darren Elliott**
Deputy Bar and Food Manager **Claire Simpson**
Duty House Managers **Charlie Revell*, Matt Wood***
Bookshop Manager **Simon David**
Assistant Bookshop Manager **Edin Suljic***
Bookshop Assistants **Nicki Welburn*, Fiona Clift***
Stage Door/Reception **Simon David*, Jon Hunter,
Paul Lovegrove, Tyrone Lucas**

Thanks to all of our box office assistants, ushers and bar staff.

+ The Associate Director post is supported by the BBC through the Gerald Chapman Fund.

* Part-time.

# We've always been happy to be less famous than our clients

Throughout our long history, Coutts has always been happy to be less famous than our clients. Clients such as Sir Henry Irving, Phineas Barnum, Bram Stoker, Charles Dickens and Frédéric Chopin to name but a few.

Coutts has a long and rich association with the performing arts, and we are still privileged to have many individuals from this arena amongst our clients. As a leading sponsor of the performing arts, Coutts is pleased and proud to support the Royal Court.

For more information about Coutts, call us on 020 7753 1851 or visit our website www.coutts.com

*Sir Henry Irving was considered to be one of the greatest actors of his day. He played a wide range of Shakespearean roles and was a good friend of Thomas Coutts' granddaughter.*

Bath, Birmingham, Bournemouth, Bristol, Cambridge, Cardiff, Eton, Guildford, Hampshire, Leeds, Liverpool, London, Manchester, Newcastle upon Tyne, Nottingham, Oxford, Tunbridge Wells.
CALLS MAY BE RECORDED

# SCENES FROM THE BACK OF BEYOND

First published in 2006 by Oberon Books Ltd
521 Caledonian Road, London N7 9RH
Tel: 020 7607 3637 / Fax: 020 7607 3629
e-mail: info@oberonbooks.com
www.oberonbooks.com

A catalogue record for this book is available from the British
Library.

ISBN: 1 84002 708 8 / 978-1-84002-708-2

Cover image: Research Studios

Printed in Great Britain by Antony Rowe Ltd, Chippenham

# Characters

BILL, 40s

HELEN, his wife, 40s

JASMINE, their daughter, 15

DAVID, a scientist, late 30s to 40s

GUY, his son, about 10

ROBBO, a neighbour, 30s to 50s

*Setting: a Sydney home around 1959*

# Scene 1

BILL  Enlightenment

Encompassing everyone

Is that fanciful

Just in the last week, I've been visited in my office by a glass fibre wizard from Ceylon, two young Indian blokes who know more about conductivity than I ever will, and a female metallurgist from Yugoslavia

In pedal-pushers

Yes

Things have certainly come on

Since the war

That dreadful lesson

Which at least proved the power, in the end, of rational people working for the common good

So that now, in 1959, I wake up in the morning feeling not bad

Because the future

The real future, the one we've all been waiting for

Where people finally understand how to be happy

*GUY in.*

Is –

(*To GUY.*) What's up

How are you doing

This is my new hi-fi

It's a mess, isn't it

But eventually, for the price of the rottenest system on the market, I'm going to have the most magnificent sound you ever heard

How about that

Are you keen on music?

Your dad's a music buff

We've spotted him at recitals in town

Why don't you take a look out the front. See if you can see him

You could have a wander about. There might be some apricots ripe. You could pick a bag of beans, for your dad

When Jasmine was about your age, she used to sit in the fowl-yard, drawing pictures of the chooks

As a matter of fact, she produced some remarkable likenesses

People have made a name for themselves painting cows

Why not chooks

*GUY off.*

He's not the most convivial

The father's an outstanding man

A scientist

And a music lover

*ROBBO in.*

ROBBO    Do you know what the little bugger did at my place

He set fire to the yard broom and he was chasing round after my kids waving it in the air and yelling, 'I'm God and I'm going to destroy the world'

I suppose they've got to get it out of their system

How about the dad, what a rat-bag

BILL    You don't know what you're talking about, Robbo

ROBBO    Why, do you know him?

BILL    I've met him

ROBBO    That must have been a privilege

Remember when they were building that house. What they must have spent. They had that architect

Jeez, and when it was finished

It was an absolute eyesore

Like something from out of space

BILL    It's contemporary. It's streamlined

ROBBO    Why do you want a house to be streamlined? Where's it going?

BILL    How about into the future

ROBBO    Straight down the pan is where it's gone

         I heard she changed the locks

         It makes you think twice though, doesn't it, about
         kicking over the traces

         I reckon one woman's enough for me

         More than enough

BILL     I tried it

ROBBO    You didn't

         Did you?

         So

         What was it like

BILL     I thought I had it all worked out. I didn't want to lie
         to Helen. I decided she and this girl could be friends

         It seemed like the rational thing

         I'd come down from the farm and Sydney was a
         hotbed of intellectual activity at the time

         Various activities, in fact

         Have you read any Jean-Paul Sartre?

ROBBO    It seems to me

         You can read Jean-Paul Sartre till the cows come
         home, it still won't make you French

BILL     I suggested to Helen the three of us have tea
         together. We lived in a flat near the Harbour in those
         days, in a marvellous old house by the waterfront
         with a frangipani perfuming the garden

ROBBO    What did she say?

BILL    She threw herself off the jetty

She was OK

The water wasn't deep there

Helen's a tall woman

That's when I realised, the beginning of rationality is knowing you can't always count on it

*JASMINE in.*

JASMINE    He's not touching my records.

Mum said he could play my records

BILL    If your mother said he / could

JASMINE    He's not coming in my room

BILL    You know the rule, Jasmine, your records get played on your record player in your / room

JASMINE    It's my *room*

BILL    He's not so bad

You need to get to know him

JASMINE    No I don't

I hate him

BILL    Any particular reason?

JASMINE    One. He's a boy

ROBBO    What's wrong with boys, eh Jasmine?

BILL    You're not a man-hater, are you

JASMINE   Mary's a man-hater. All she and mum ever talk
          about is how they hate men. If they hate them so
          much, how come that's all they ever talk about

BILL   Jasmine

          When people are in trouble, it doesn't always
          happen at everyone's convenience or when you're
          feeling ready to be kind. You still have to –

JASMINE   Why do you

BILL   Why?

          I don't know

          When I was a kid about his age, our friends had this
          holiday shack

          It was set back from the beach behind the dunes,
          and the grass around the shack was adorned in all
          directions with cow dung

          I remember standing in the doorway thinking, this is
          a bit unsavoury

          When suddenly the father of the family picks up a
          cow-pat and buzzes it at the mother and she catches
          it and buzzes it back at him

          And the next thing that happens, the father, the
          mother and me and kids all together are running
          around chucking cow-pats at each other

          Having the time of our lives

          The weather was so dry down there, they'd dried out
          like meringues

          They were the best thing to throw I ever threw

And it struck me with the force of a vision. These
people knew something my family and I didn't know

How to live

I've been hoping ever since it's something you can
learn

And pass on, so the microcosm feeds into the
macrocosm and the macrocosm feeds back into the

Do you see what I mean?

It's finding how to make things, I don't know

It's finding things are really OK

JASMINE   So

You're asking me to lie

BILL   Jasmine

You'll discover as you go through life, sincerity isn't
always the thing that's chiefly required

*JASMINE off.*

BILL   I need a beer

*BILL and ROBBO off. After a moment, GUY comes in.
Then JASMINE.*

JASMINE   Do you want to play these

*She holds out a set of pick-up sticks but GUY doesn't take
them. She scatters them and starts picking them up.*

Who's your teacher?

When I was a first year we had Mrs Barker

She made us do breathing

You know when someone says 'Breathe' and you suddenly think 'Help, what do I do'

GUY     That's a girl's game

JASMINE     Can't you play it

GUY     Watch this

*GUY gathers the pick-up sticks and presses the points into his leg.*

JASMINE     That's really stupid

GUY     It doesn't hurt

JASMINE     I know

*GUY presses the sticks into JASMINE's leg.*

That doesn't hurt

*GUY presses harder.*

That doesn't hurt

*GUY presses harder.*

GUY     Does that hurt?

JASMINE     No

*GUY presses harder.*

This is good fun, but I'm going now, all right

*JASMINE off. After a while, GUY off. HELEN and DAVID in.*

HELEN    Guy?

Where's he got to

He's no trouble, honestly

DAVID    Do you think Mary's all right?

HELEN    I'll tell her you asked

DAVID    I mean, in the head

Do you think my son's all right with her?

HELEN    Perhaps you should have thought of that sooner

DAVID    Yes

I fell for someone

If I'd thought it would break up our marriage

HELEN    Why didn't you think that

DAVID    Mary wasn't meant to find out

She discovered my vitamins. 'This array of medications,' as she called it. I said I was trying to get fit, and for some reason, bang, she knew

HELEN    So you'd have had your cake and eaten it

DAVID    Yes

The bad thing is

Some of the best times I had with Joan were when we were agonising to each other over what we were doing to our loved ones. It seemed to inspire us in some unfortunate way

HELEN     I'm sure we've all done things we're not proud of

DAVID     Yes

Have you?

HELEN     As a matter of fact I haven't

DAVID     Joan wanted a husband. And I was one. Till I met her. When Mary threw me out I ceased to be that person. So that was the end of Joan. I don't know what I am now. I don't know if I'm even a person at all, I feel like some fly-away thing, some puffball

I'm living in absolute squalor

HELEN     I can imagine

*BILL enters.*

BILL     It's good to see you

I know all about you, of course

DAVID     That sounds alarming

*ROBBO in.*

BILL     And this is Robbo

ROBBO     Number 22

We can see your house from the patio

It's quite a landmark

DAVID   Thank you

It might not be mine for much longer, the way things are going

ROBBO   Yeah

We heard

What do you do for a crust, David?

DAVID   I work at Lucas Heights

BILL   He's an atomic scientist

ROBBO   And what does that entail exactly

DAVID   I'm mainly concerned with attempting to hit invisible particles with other invisible particles

ROBBO   Sounds tricky

I suppose, if you miss, who's to know

So when's the next Hiroshima

DAVID   What do you do?

ROBBO   I sell carports

It's not exactly rocket science

BILL   I've heard you speak

Last year. You were talking about the High Flux Isotope Reactor

Most enlightening

The Institute of Mining and Metallurgy

DAVID   I didn't know anyone round here was –

You should have introduced yourself

BILL    I did

DAVID   So

We meet again

HELEN   Guy?

There you are

Here he is

Dad's here

DAVID   Hullo son

Come and say hullo

What's up

I'm sorry I'm late

I didn't find your mother's note

It fell down out of sight when I was kicking the door

I hurt my foot

I'm sorry we were late back last time

Did you get your roast dinner?

GUY     Yeah

DAVID   Pretty extravagant

For two

Was it good?

GUY     Yeah

DAVID   So your mother wasn't angry

GUY     She was crying

DAVID    Yes

         What shall we do today

  GUY    You said

DAVID    What did I say

  GUY    You said we were going to the beach

DAVID    Did your mother remember to give you your
         swimmers?

  GUY    Yeah

DAVID    We'll just have to nip back for mine

HELEN    In this traffic

         You're the other side of town

  BILL   I'll lend you some

DAVID    Thanks, do you mean it?

         I completely forgot

         I feel like a worm

         *HELEN off.*

DAVID    How's school

         What have you been up to

  GUY    Are we going to be late back?

DAVID    Why

  GUY    I don't want to go to the beach

DAVID    Don't worry

Stop worrying

We don't want you turning into a worrier

Like your mother

How have you been

Have you been good

What does your mother say

GUY        She says I don't care and I'm like you

*HELEN in, with swimming trunks.*

BILL        What are those

HELEN        The old ones

DAVID        Thanks. Thanks very much

HELEN        Don't worry about returning them

BILL        Come and have a feed

Tonight, when you've dropped him off

DAVID        Are you sure?

BILL        We'd be delighted, wouldn't we Helen

DAVID        Thanks. I'll see you later then. I'll bring these back

*DAVID and GUY off.*

HELEN        What on earth

BILL        What

ROBBO        I'll see you later

*ROBBO off.*

BILL     That's OK, isn't it?

        We see enough of Mary

        Every time I go in the kitchen she's there at the gin bottle

HELEN     What am I going to say to her?

BILL     It's our house, kiddo

        But if you don't like him

        After all

        I don't like her

HELEN     Mary comes here because we haven't taken sides

BILL     So she gets the run of the kitchen and he gets the bum's rush because we haven't taken sides

        What's the matter

        Are you frightened for your virtue?

        All you women reckon he's some kind of Lothario just because he

HELEN     Invite him then

BILL     Still, if Mary's got you brainwashed to that extent

HELEN     I said, invite him

BILL     Kiddo, if you don't feel you can cope

HELEN     Go ahead

BILL     If you want me to call it off, I'll call it off

HELEN   What, and make out it's all my fault

BILL    Did I say that?

HELEN   Anyway, we can't put him off now

BILL    If that's the price of domestic harmony

HELEN   You've asked him, we'll have to go through with it

BILL    Well then

        If you're sure

        He's an interesting bloke

HELEN   Would you abandon your wife and child?

BILL    What?

HELEN   Well? Would you?

BILL    I must say, kiddo

        You're getting a bit bourgeois in your old age

HELEN   Who are you calling bourgeois? I live on a wage

BILL    My wage

HELEN   I subsist on your wage. That makes me decidedly working class

BILL    The logic is impeccable

HELEN   Who's logical? At least I don't work for capitalists

BILL    You just live off the proceeds!

HELEN   If I were logical, I wouldn't even be here

BILL    Where would you be? Manning the barricades? That I'd like to see

Don't worry, you're safe from that. What are we, one per cent of one per cent

HELEN   You have no idea how I feel

About anything

BILL   It's not for want of being told

HELEN   Of course, you believe in free love, as I recall

BILL   And why not?

I hear it's practised in Russia

There's more than one way of boosting productivity, old girl

HELEN   You call yourself a Marxist. You'd never have even heard of Marx if it hadn't been for me. When I met you, you thought a Molotov cocktail was a cocktail

Anyway, Russia is old hat

In China, they discourage sexual activity

BILL   Not only in China

HELEN   It says in *China Reconstructs*, they can now amputate people's limbs using nothing but acupuncture

BILL   Helen, they may not be giving the whole picture

HELEN   It's illustrated

Chairman Mao is embarking on a Great Leap Forward

BILL   So they haven't amputated his

HELEN   The sexes in China live apart until they're thirty. They're happy, constructive, devoid of personal vanity, they work hard, they eat a hearty meal

of noodles and fresh vegetables at night, their
complexions are clear, their eyes are bright and they
sing

BILL     What have they got to sing about

         'We shall build a dam on the mighty River Yangtse'
         or some such thing

HELEN    So maybe I'm not as neurotic as you think

BILL     Here we go

HELEN    I'm not the one who said it

BILL     Can't we just have one day when we don't wind up
         fighting

HELEN    Who's fighting? I'm stating facts

         You're oversexed

         It's not as if you show me any tenderness

         You do it for your health

         It's as automatic as opening the fridge

BILL     It's interesting you should make that comparison

HELEN    Has it ever occurred to you, I might be with the
         wrong man?

BILL     Yes. Frequently

HELEN    Of course men who attach extreme importance to
         sex are often closet homosexuals

         Is that why you want to invite him?

BILL     Oh for Christ's sake

HELEN    If you were one of them, at least I'd get a night's sleep occasionally. You're like an animal

*JASMINE in.*

BILL    A little contretemps

*JASMINE off. HELEN off.*

Any marriage, even a happy one

So-called

Bears the scars of thousands of years of social deformity

Any kind of flowering people manage to achieve in this society is bound to be less than complete

We built this house in 1950

It made better sense than renting, and you get used to the journey into town

The procession of husbands to the station

It's fatal to walk at the same speed as anyone else or you might wind up doing the whole walk with them. For the next thirty years

I used to carry Jasmine down here to watch them putting up the timber frame

We were the first ones here to plant native trees

A bit of a guilt offering, after the bulldozers

Of course, Helen and I are opposed to the private ownership of land

But, pending the revolution…

I think he's much maligned

Scientists are generally misunderstood

For the simple reason that science is generous

Scientists just want to find things out, and share them around

That mystifies people

Most of life, as people know it, isn't generous

So people think anyone who is generous must be up to something

Science as a profession is sunny natured, you could almost say angelic

Not in all its applications perhaps

But in its creative heart

The man who invented the wheel didn't have to hurt anyone to do it

Epicurus said it

As people learn to understand, they'll cease to suffer from ridiculous notions and irrational fears, and then they won't feel the need to tear each other to bits

Admittedly, he said it some time ago

300 BC

But this is the age of science

We're making such advances

In disease control, efficient agriculture, mass production, aeronautics, nuclear power

Religion, capitalism, nationalism are all on the way out

Sickness, toil, poverty and war are simply going to go

There's going to be enough of everything, easily manufactured and harvested

No more long hours

And once people are free of material pressures

They'll become beautiful

## Scene 2

*BILL, HELEN, JASMINE, DAVID after dinner. Irmgard Seefried, 'Shepherd on the Rock'.*

DAVID    She's got my record collection

BILL    I'd make divorce available on request

I'd do away with all the accusations and the stigma

HELEN    I wonder if anyone would actually stay married

DAVID    I think Mary and I were already the height of depravity, in people's eyes round here

One evening, I washed out my walking socks, and was pegging them up to dry

Mary was on the terrace with a sherry in her hand. She heard Janis next door say to Clem, 'What are they doing now?'

And Clem replied, 'Mr Nair is hanging out the washing, and Mrs Nair is sitting drinking wine'

BILL    Robbo next door to us is the salt of the earth but he's not the most erudite of minds

I asked him one day what he thought about Indo-China. He said 'I don't know Bill. What's outdoor china anyway?'

Beyond him it's the Italians

HELEN    I'd extend the hand of friendship, but that's not the part they want to hold

BILL    Surely the working class are entitled to grab your bum on the bus from time to time

HELEN    Please

They're not working class

BILL    They work, don't they?

HELEN    You know perfectly well they're peasant landowners, dyed-in-the-wool reactionaries

BILL    I stand corrected

HELEN    And the women. Dressed in black from head to toe and hissing through their teeth at anyone in a sun-frock

And I'm the one who feels embarrassed, me, in my own country. Heaven knows the last thing I want is to be working eighteen hours a day picking tomatoes

But they seem so

Real

I wonder what it's like

The problem with Australia is all this good fortune

DAVID    People say Australians are complacent. I think
they're also afraid. I think they're doing well
but they can't believe their luck and they've got
an awful feeling they don't deserve it. And they
vote for Menzies because when they look at his
imperturbable, British looking, fat-of-the-land
countenance, they're able to forget they're living
on the far side of the world, in a country they stole
from its inhabitants, on the fringes of the world's
biggest desert. Not voting for Menzies would be like
admitting your floral hat is full of flying ants, or your
rugby field's turned to concrete in the drought, or
the dust storms have engulfed your topiary, or your
nice red brickwork's got funnel-web spiders in it.
And so by extension a vote for the other side is like
voting in favour of bushfires or poisonous snakes, it's
like letting in the nothingness or even worse the guilt
that's waiting out there in the bush at the end of your
copiously watered backyard

BILL    Speaking of which. I won't be a moment

*BILL off.*

HELEN    He's peeing under the apricot tree

Marriage

I do love him

For years and years I never even noticed, his ears
stick out. He was on the platform one night at the
Parent Teachers Association, and suddenly I saw the
light shining through them

It's complicated, isn't it

To tell you the absolute truth, there are times when I think you and Mary might have done the right thing

JASMINE    Mum

DAVID    You'd be surprised how many happily married people have said that to me recently. Since we broke up I seem to have become some sort of marital lightning rod

HELEN    Do you know what I'd like?

I'd like a little flat near the harbour, and never to have to pluck another chook

It's a fact, make of it what you will. Most of Sydney's politically conscious people live within the sound of the bells on the masts of the Yacht Club

All this suburban utopian food-growing

I was never meant to grow my own food

I'm from Melbourne

*BILL in.*

Excuse me a moment

*HELEN off.*

BILL    She's never been in favour of people being happy

Because if people perversely insist on feeling OK, there'll be no revolution, and she wants one. That's why she joined the Parent Teachers Association. And the film club. So that when the time comes, she'll be in place

I think she really believes that

Whatever she hasn't got, that's what she wants

Even if it's misery

As far as she's concerned, the world's all wrong and her vocation lies in telling me to put it right

She grows these bloody rhododendrons. Why does anyone grow bloody rhododendrons in this climate? She grows these bloody rhododendrons and they die. She knows each one by name. She sits beside its deathbed sprinkling water on it. White Pearl. 'Have you seen what's happened to my poor White Pearl?'

It's neurotic

Marriage

To tell you the truth, I think you might have done the right thing

JASMINE   Dad

DAVID   So I've been told

BILL   She's fundamentally afraid of pleasure

She's from Melbourne

*HELEN in.*

HELEN   I suppose he's also told you I'm neurotic

DAVID   It's a compliment, surely

HELEN   Coming from him

I think you're right

BILL   We've got this Yank at work

Visiting

I don't really have much to do with him

My field is radio parts

It's pretty run-of-the-mill

The company's got its fingers in a lot of other pies

Rocketry, et cetera

DAVID  Yes

It's a big company

BILL  I sincerely hope the rockets are pointing into space

Although the fact remains I don't know where the bloody things are pointing. Should I ask. Would I be told. Do pigs fly

How does anyone ever manage to do anything that's unconditionally good?

Don't you think, if people didn't have children for the usual reasons

They'd do it as their only possible shot at building paradise

I look at Jasmine and I think, yes, at least we had this measure of power to do our best, and we did

But otherwise

We're communists, for God's sake

Lapsed ones

The party was going a bit haywire

They purged someone from the ranks for failing to condemn Donald Duck

We felt that was excessive

Possibly

Besides, I needed the job

HELEN   Working for a giant American company that makes rockets

BILL   Anyway this Yank

He hailed me as a fellow-scientist so I asked him what he studied

Time and motion, he replied

Oh, I said, like Einstein

He looked bemused

Ever since he came, he's been holed up in the ping-pong room writing reports

About shift-working

I said to him, what's the point? What you save on keeping the machinery going, you lose on wages at time-and-a-half or double-time, because those are the union rates and they're fair, when you think of the damage to the individual's patterns of sleep and personal life, not to mention the increase in accidents and

All he said to that was, the world's running faster all the time

He reckons the workforce in a country like this one doesn't get it because they're all too busy enjoying life

He and Helen would see eye to eye on that one

HELEN    It couldn't be more different

I want progress

BILL     He says that as well

Isn't enjoying life what progress is supposed to be for?

In his view, enjoying life is supposed to be the goal, therefore, it can't be allowed to become the reality. Because if it's the reality, there's no goal

He said, if people didn't have the constant pressure to better themselves, why would they do anything?

I said, how about curiosity. Pleasure. Creativity. Social interaction. Self-respect. Altruism. Love

I don't think he quite bought that

But it's ridiculous

We've got all this labour-saving equipment which is meant to be saving labour

Reducing working hours for God's sake

And the only thing an idiot like him can think of doing with it

Is to sack half the workforce and keep the rest toiling like slaves

You're fortunate

With your ability

DAVID    Yes

I love my work

I marvel at what I see

Infinitesimal inevitable events, deep within the visible changeable world

I live every day with this vision which is fresh as the dawn

Untainted by the accidents of the day, the human strife

And as I contemplate those hidden coherences

Human behaviour seems utterly remote and absurd to me

The Russians are building a whole new city devoted to science

In Siberia

A place called the Golden Valley, outside Novosibirsk

They've given it the name Akademgorodok

They're setting up an institute for each discipline

Nuclear Physics, Hydrodynamics, Catalysis

With an Institute of Abstract Mathematics at the centre, so all the disciplines will converse

In absolute freedom, apparently

It's going to put Russia right out in front

Scientists are already moving there from all over the USSR. Spacious accommodation is being built among the birch trees. It has its own schools and shopping complexes and its own elite university

They're bringing sand to make a beach on the River Ob

HELEN    And we're stuck here in this pointless paradise

It's frustrating

When you look at the developments under socialism

JASMINE    How can you look at them?

HELEN    What, darling?

JASMINE    How can you look at the developments under socialism, when no one can go to Russia and no one can leave

HELEN    People go to Russia

People are invited

The Russians look after everything, they even give you an interpreter

JASMINE    That's so you can't go where you want

HELEN    Russia isn't like here

JASMINE    Why isn't it

HELEN    How do they know if people will understand

With all the saboteurs and sceptics there are

The whole capitalist world wants to see the end of Russia

It's no wonder they don't trust anyone

JASMINE    They have prison camps

HELEN    Who's been telling you these fairy-tales

JASMINE    It's on the news

HELEN    The news

Don't tell me you believe the news

JASMINE     You have it on

Why do you have it on?

Just so you can look down your nose at it?

HELEN     And why not

Journalists will say anything their right-wing bosses
tell them to

I was in public relations don't forget

JASMINE     For a corset company

HELEN     No

Foundation garments

There's anti-Soviet propaganda being churned out
all the time

JASMINE     What if it's true

HELEN     How would you know

JASMINE     How would you

BILL     Jasmine, does it make any sense to you, that a
regime whose whole ideology revolves around doing
away with oppression should be putting people in
labour camps just like some fascist state?

JASMINE     Yeah but dad

There are lots of things that don't make any sense
and they still seem to –

HELEN     The testimony's coming from sworn opponents to
the regime

JASMINE     If I thought they had prison camps, I'd be a sworn
            opponent to the regime

HELEN       I refuse to believe the Russians would do such
            a thing. They're idealistic people, incredibly
            courageous. If there's such a thing as labour camps,
            Jasmine, why do we never hear about it from anyone
            on the Left?

JASMINE     If we did hear about it from anyone on the Left,
            you'd say they couldn't be on the Left

HELEN       Well. They couldn't be

JASMINE     I'm just trying to keep an open mind

HELEN       I'm sorry, Jasmine, but in terms of the ideological
            struggle being waged, keeping an open mind can be
            tantamount to supporting the enemy

JASMINE     I'm not

BILL        Of course we need to keep an open mind. So long as
            that includes a certain level of scepticism about these
            so-called reports of labour camps

HELEN       I never thought I'd see the day when a daughter of
            mine would be a capitalist revisionist

JASMINE     I'm not a capitalist

            I don't know why anyone's a capitalist

            Capitalists are just show-offs

            But Khrushchev and Mao, with their chests stuck out

            Are they your idea of a communist?

## Scene 3

*BILL, later that night.*

BILL     I've thought those things

But even if they're

There are bound to be abuses when everything's being turned upside down

The prize could be so great

If socialism's all wrong, then where do we

And what have we been

The lamb was pretty much of a triumph

With a decent red, and larded with garlic, you could almost be in the South of France with the artists

Sydney's got artists

I don't know that crowd, but you can see them if you go to Kings Cross. There's a sort of coffee bar

And a wide selection of ladies of the night

A mate of mine used to work in a bank in Kings Cross, and the prostitutes used to bank their money there. Wads of cash

He was writing out a form for one of them, a big peroxide blonde

He said to her, 'And what's your occupation, please?'

'Sticking straws through the holes in a wire mattress,' she replied

I love Sydney

We've never tried to dictate to her

She can say what she wants

Anyway

Family life


## Scene 4

*A few nights later. DAVID, JASMINE.*

DAVID Oh God!

Oh God

What have I done

JASMINE It's all right

DAVID You didn't tell me you were / a

JASMINE What did you think I was?

DAVID I suppose I just thought kids these days are –

How old are you?

JASMINE Fifteen

DAVID Oh God

JASMINE I wanted to lose it

DAVID You're fifteen

JASMINE I was waiting for the right person

DAVID Who

JASMINE You

DAVID     Jasmine, I don't think we should rush into anything

JASMINE   It's a bit of a strange time to say that

DAVID     I couldn't stop

          I should have stopped

          Why didn't you stop me?

JASMINE   I didn't think you wanted me to stop you

DAVID     Was it all right

JASMINE   Yeah

          I'll get used to it

DAVID     This shouldn't have happened

JASMINE   What do you mean?

DAVID     I'm your parents' generation

          Not that I want to be

          I can't tell you how glad I am to be out of all that
          mess

          But I'm not exactly young and handsome

JASMINE   It doesn't matter

DAVID     Thanks

JASMINE   Other things are more important

DAVID     Yes

          What things

JASMINE   Compatibility

DAVID     What

JASMINE    I'm going to be a geologist

DAVID      Oh

           Wonderful

JASMINE    I've collected rocks ever since I was a kid

DAVID      Have you

JASMINE    Dad showed me

           Dad would have liked to be a geologist really

           And when I was little he'd say something to me
           like, 'This is chalcedony', and I'd think, wow, this is
           chalcedony

           You know how kids are

DAVID      I'm trying to think of you as a geologist

JASMINE    But I've always taken more after dad

DAVID      What would you do about field trips?

           You can't make a career in geology without going
           out on field trips

JASMINE    I go fossicking with dad sometimes or out where
           someone's dynamiting something and we can pick
           up some samples. I like being out in the bush. I
           can cook damper and everything. Dad and I have
           walked in the Blue Mountains. People die there. It's
           so beautiful. The gullies are so deep and cool and
           the trees are gigantic

DAVID      It's just that men in the circumstances of a field
           trip tend to be pretty free and easy. I don't know if
           they'd welcome having a woman along. From the
           point of view of decency

Jasmine, I could be arrested

This can't happen again

JASMINE    Don't you want it to?

DAVID    It's not that

Please

Jasmine

What would your father say?

JASMINE    He wouldn't mind

He likes you

DAVID    He wouldn't like me, if he could see us now

JASMINE    Dad says you're a proper scientist. He's never done research

DAVID    I've never discovered anything

It's recently been found that brain cells don't renew themselves beyond the age of twenty-five

I'm forty

JASMINE    I wish he wouldn't be ashamed of it though

DAVID    Cannon fodder

JASMINE    You?

Don't be ridiculous

Have you got a cigarette?

DAVID    You're too young to smoke

*He gives her a cigarette.*

JASMINE    What would they say at school

This beats Latin

BILL    (*Off.*) Jasmine is that a cigarette I can smell?

*BILL in.*

Jasmine?

What the hell are you doing?

DAVID    I

*BILL attacks DAVID who retreats. HELEN in.*

BILL    You

HELEN    Oh no

No

You

And

How could you

In this house

We were at a parents' evening!

JASMINE    We're not ashamed

Are we

HELEN    You've broken the law!

JASMINE    You don't believe in the law

HELEN    What?

JASMINE    You believe in the withering away of the state

HELEN    Don't drag politics into this

JASMINE    You're the one talking about the law!

I just want to live my life

HELEN    Well you've made quite a start

You're a child. It's not normal

It's sick. You're sick

Talk to her, Bill

Your father wants to say something

BILL    Actually

I started at thirteen

HELEN    Right

At least we know whose child she is

JASMINE    Boys can do what they want

HELEN    Boys have nothing to lose

JASMINE    The sexes are equal, you said

HELEN    I said, equal but different

Of course I believe in equality of opportunity, but

JASMINE    This was an opportunity

HELEN    I never suggested you simply jump into bed with someone

Let alone use the floor

He's old enough to be your father

JASMINE   What's age got to do with it?

          You said it's the person that counts

HELEN     The person

          You don't even know him

JASMINE   Yes I do

BILL      Jasmine. Of course we want you to be true to
          yourself

HELEN     Not if she's like this

BILL      She has to have feelings

HELEN     That's what self-control is for

JASMINE   You're not talking about self-control. You're talking
          about your control

          You want to stop me from being happy

          Because you're not

          And you're not young and I am

          That really gives you the shits

HELEN     You vicious little bitch

BILL      Let's all calm down

          It's been a disastrous encounter

HELEN     You

          You invited him

          (*To DAVID.*) As for you

DAVID     I'm so sorry. I just –

BILL   Shut up

DAVID  I'm so sorry

HELEN  I think you'd better leave

DAVID  Yes of course

JASMINE Where are you going

DAVID  Jasmine, I –

JASMINE If he goes, I'll go too

DAVID  No!

HELEN  If you go with him, Jasmine, I'll call the police

JASMINE Call them

DAVID  Jasmine!

JASMINE It's the only real thing that's ever happened

     The rest is just grey

     I love him

BILL   Just because you've

     You think he

     You have no idea what men are / like

DAVID  I love Jasmine

BILL   Don't be ridiculous

DAVID  Do you think I'd just –

     If I didn't love her, what sort of man would I be

BILL   I'll tell you what / sort of

DAVID     It's the most honest thing I've ever done

          What standards are you judging me by?

          I'm sure they're not yours

          I'm asking for your daughter's hand in marriage

          You'll want to think about it

BILL      No, I don't

DAVID     She'll soon be old enough

          We'll wait

          Won't we, Jasmine

          I'll go now

          *DAVID off.*

JASMINE   Dad?


# Scene 5

*BILL comes home from work. He puts down his bag, puts some music on, gets a drink, sits, takes his shoes off, lies back and listens to the music.*

*HELEN enters with cups of tea. HELEN sits watching BILL listening. Eventually BILL gives up and turns the music off.*

HELEN     The Chinese would soon deal with him

          They know what to do with intellectuals

Send him to break rocks

Say what you like, in China, our daughter would have been a different girl

It says in *China Reconstructs* –

BILL    I've had it up to here with you and your bloody *China Reconstructs*

I doubt that Chairman Mao is going to help us in this matter

HELEN   How was your day

BILL    How was yours

HELEN   I should have seen it coming

When she wanted those black jeans you let her have

She's our daughter

Not some jitterbugging Hell's Angel

That whole black jeans thing is American inspired

BILL    Just suppose

HELEN   What

BILL    Love at first sight

It happens

HELEN   Have you finally gone stark staring mad?

BILL    She's a thinker

HELEN   Is that relevant?

BILL    He's led a rarefied existence

She may be destined to become a scientist of similar calibre

HELEN   You think she'll catch it, like measles

Or some other complaint

Bill

Since when did any man

BILL   Our daughter is worthy of

HELEN   Our daughter

The one woman exempt from the disgrace of being female

That's how you see her

As far as you're concerned, she's almost an honorary man

This wild behaviour

What did you expect, teaching her carpentry

And home brewing

BILL   I thought we were bringing her up to be free of the

HELEN   Yes

But

Oh Bill

Ever since we built this house I've dreamt of her wedding in the garden, with the trees all grown up

A radiant confident young woman in a beautiful white veil, carrying a bouquet of rhododendrons

Marrying an equally radiant, gentle, considerate young man who's confident and sensible and

strong and who works in international relations or
anthropology

BILL     It's one small incident

Maybe it will all blow over


# Scene 6

*BILL, DAVID, HELEN.*

HELEN    You're very punctual

DAVID    It's the traffic

Has Mary been

HELEN    No

DAVID    She's blown this thing up out of all proportion

HELEN    Well

It's quite an important thing

DAVID    Yes of course

So

How are you

It's a little-known fact

This furniture is flowing

It's changing shape

As the molecules

Flow

If we were to look again at this furniture

In several million years

Everything being equal

It would have flowed down

The legs flowing into the feet

The feet spreading into the floor

Salvador Dali knew what he was doing

It's happening now

Everything around us that we perceive as solid

Walls, window frames, whisky glasses

Is slowly melting down

*JASMINE in.*

JASMINE    I'm ready


# Scene 7

*BILL in the middle of the night. HELEN in.*

HELEN    At least we know who she's with

It's just that knowing who she's with makes it worse

Come back to bed

I may have been critical

Can't we just comfort each other?

I know I'm not always consistent

Is that any reason to write someone off?

Bill

I'm here

Even if I'm only here to be hurt

It's as if the very fact that I'm here to be hurt makes you barely able to stand my proximity

And that's what hurts me

But how can I be here, without being here to be hurt?

I just wish you didn't make me feel like a permanently inflamed sore thumb

One that's been hit by a hammer

Not that you've ever hit me with a hammer

Or said much to me about what you're really thinking

But that in itself somehow feels like a permanent hammer blow

Leaving me permanently inflamed, and that's why everything I say and do is too much, I'm either too antagonistic because I'm trying to clear the air, or I'm too effusive because I'm casting myself into a void

BILL        I said to Don

The Yank, the time and motion man

I said, skip the shift-working

Who wants their sleep ruined for life?

He replied, I'll tell you who

People who don't have unions

This is Australia

We've got the highest standard of living in the world, and the best unions

I happen to believe the two things are related

We've learned to look after each other in this country. We don't torment each other for the sake of every last red cent

In his eyes, that's regrettable

The fact is

He's come to Sydney to break the back of the unions

I'm supposed to applaud him for this

It seems there are countries where the company makes double the profit

They want to continue in Sydney but 'only if they can afford to'

Which implies that, in whatever country the unions manage to find their feet, a company like ours will pull out the rug and locate somewhere else

At that rate, there'll come a time when governments start closing unions down 'in the national interest'

He told me research has shown that, although people working at night start out by being less productive and more accident prone, eventually the social and sensory deprivation they experience drives them deeper into their work and they become as productive as by day

He said you can't argue with science

Science

Apparently a workforce that can see out of a window
is less productive than a workforce facing a wall

He wants to brick the windows up

The unions will fight him into the ground

Maybe that's what he's after, an excuse to close the
place

I've been thinking, I ought to leave

There are other jobs

Bugger the pension rights

What do you think

On the other hand

If I stay, maybe I can talk to both sides

Negotiate

Intervene for once

It isn't like world affairs, up there out of reach

Politics flying around like storm clouds

And me a tiny figure brandishing my spear at them

This is down here on the ground

So should I quit

Or should I wait

See how things develop

Shit

That's what I always say

What am I going to do

Helen?

HELEN    I saw

All the generations of man on a cold grey floor under a cold grey sky

Blind and struggling, like bait

It all looked as cold as Dante imagined the lowest circle of hell to be

Not even a splash of red blood to brighten it up

I sometimes feel as if my own tears are the only warm thing left to hide in

People say, it's not personal, it's business

Business is personal

BILL    Yes

HELEN    It's so unfair

If you'd gone to university

BILL    I couldn't go to university

Dad bought that bloody farm, it was all hands on deck

HELEN    The old shit

BILL    I couldn't just leave him / to

HELEN    Your father never did anything for anyone in his life

BILL    By the time he'd finished running the place into the ground I had to settle for night school

And as it happens, I fell on my feet

HELEN   I wish there was something I could

I don't know enough to

Maybe you're right, maybe I don't want to know enough

But why should I have to, why should anyone have to

Know those things

In a proper world it wouldn't be needed

When I try to look at certain things I just can't see straight

I can't look at them

You know that

If only there'd been some other / way

BILL   We wanted to get married

Have a house

A child

## Scene 8

*ROBBO and BILL.*

ROBBO   What's this picture you're dragging me to

*BILL hands him a piece of paper.*

'Fishermen wresting a living from the seas of southern Italy are caught in a bitter struggle against exploitation'

That sounds pretty powerful

The boot's on the other foot in my experience. When Huey takes me out at Nambucca, I pay him a small fortune and he eats my banana sandwiches as well

Last time we were out, we caught a shark. I said to him, 'What are you going to do with the shark, Huey?' 'Shark?' he says. 'That's flathead'

You should always check your fish and chips

You might find yourself eating a fingernail or a belt buckle

BILL    There's some cinema vérité coming up

ROBBO    What's that

BILL    It's French

ROBBO    You old perv

BILL    As I explained

A bunch of us founded film club so people round here would have some sort of alternative to Hollywood

ROBBO    Yeah, you said

BILL    There's one showing a month

ROBBO    One showing, eh

BILL    At the scout hall

ROBBO   The scout hall, yeah

BILL    We share it with the scouts, the guides, the voluntary brigade of firefighters, and various possums and moths

But it has a certain rustic charm

ROBBO   Yeah

Good on you

I saw Jasmine yesterday

Heading for the station in her heels

You're modern people

I guess that helps

BILL    It doesn't help at all

ROBBO   I guess not

But there you go

She's been brought up with a whole lot of modern ideas

BILL    Plenty of kids go off the rails without being exposed to the world of the intellect

ROBBO   Yeah but

Why risk it

BILL    I'm surprised you're coming to the film with us

If that's your assessment of twentieth-century culture

ROBBO   I'm not worried

I reckon I'm immune to it

BILL    We persuaded them to come to a civilised agreement

        She can see him weekends if she does all her school-
        work

ROBBO   Yeah

        Personally, I'd knock his block off

BILL    What are we going to do? Lock her up?

        He's failed to respect our wishes

        Maybe they're not worth respecting

        I believe in science

        The way he's behaved

        I feel as if I'd walked towards the Buddha-like
        incarnation of science that shines on my horizon

        And been hit by a thousand volts, to the sound of
        echoing laughter

        I feel like nobody

        You know how it is when daughters wilt

        You think they're going to die like a sick shrub

        I remember the Sunday before it all started

        She and I walked through the bush along the creek
        to Brown's Waterhole, and I caught a freshwater
        crayfish this big. In a deep quiet pool

        I caught it with a bit of meat from the sandwiches,
        like we did when I was a boy

        I was thoroughly pleased with myself. I wanted to
        boil it in the billy straight away. There's nothing
        more delicious

She was sitting on a flat bit of rock staring into the
creek, white in the face, and I could see the animal's
life story going through her mind, the years in the
tranquil brown depths and then the terrible end

I couldn't stop myself. I put the thing back in the
creek

His intentions are honourable

ROBBO    What does Helen say

BILL    I don't care what she says

When Jasmine and he get settled

Helen and I might call it a day, I don't know

ROBBO    You wouldn't

BILL    We just get on each other's nerves

ROBBO    So

You're married

BILL    Jasmine will be OK

They'll go to all the subscription concerts

ROBBO    It's a feather in your cap

If you look at it that way

BILL    Do you think I'm happy about it?

ROBBO    No

How could you be

BILL    She's sixteen in two months. Why worry about some
fig-leaf of legality

As lesser mortals do

*HELEN in.*

HELEN     What if she's there

BILL      What if she is

          (*To ROBBO.*) Mary knows

ROBBO     Everyone knows

BILL      Everyone?

ROBBO     It's the number one topic

HELEN     I'm not going!

BILL      He doesn't mean that literally

ROBBO     Don't I just

HELEN     I'm staying home

BILL      What are you scared of? Our friends?

          So am I

          But surely a united front

          *HELEN off.*

BILL      Helen

          *BILL goes after HELEN.*

ROBBO     Are you coming to see the picture?

          *GUY enters.*

GUY       It's not a picture

ROBBO     What is it

GUY       It's a film

ROBBO     Oh. It's a film

          Are you coming to see the film?

GUY       I don't like films. I only like pictures

ROBBO     What sort of pictures do you like

GUY       Cowboy pictures

ROBBO     Cowboy pictures, eh

GUY       Do you like cowboy pictures?

ROBBO     To tell you the truth, I'm not that mad about them

GUY       Don't you like cowboy pictures?

ROBBO     They're a bit violent, aren't they?

GUY       Are you scared?

          You don't have to be scared

          It's not real

ROBBO     I think that's what scares me

GUY       Don't you like it when an arrow shoots the cowboy,
          tchk

ROBBO     I can take it or leave it, to be honest

GUY       Don't you like when the cowboys are shooting the
          Indians on the cliff and they're falling one by one,
          dwooo, dwooo, dwooo

ROBBO     Each to his own

GUY       And when the fort's on fire and the cowboy's back's
          on fire, and when they scalp them and there's blood

ROBBO     I guess I just don't have the innocence of youth

*BILL in.*

BILL      We'd better get a move on

ROBBO     Yeah

          The mozzies will be biting

*After a while, JASMINE in.*

GUY       Mum's going to tell on you

          She's going to tell the school

JASMINE   What's she going to tell them

GUY       She's going to tell the police

JASMINE   Tell the police then

          Tell them all about it

          Then your dad will go to gaol

GUY       You think dad's going to marry you

JASMINE   Do I

GUY       You do, don't you, don't you

JASMINE   What if I do

GUY       Dad will never marry you

JASMINE   I'm sorry your dad walked out but it's not my fault

He won't come back, that's for sure

GUY          You're a slut

JASMINE      Do you know what the atom bomb is?

GUY          Yeah

JASMINE      And the hydrogen bomb is even bigger

GUY          So

JASMINE      Do you ever think about them?

GUY          No

JASMINE      One atom bomb wiped out a city

GUY          They were Japs

JASMINE      America's got a whole lot of atom bombs

             And England has

             And Russia, and China

             And it's all wired up so if anyone fires one bomb, the
             rest will be fired automatically

             And guess what. There are so many bombs, they'll
             blow the whole world up, they'll blow up your mum
             and your dad and you and me and that stringy-bark
             tree and the railway station and all the trees and all
             the animals and everything that lives and there'll be
             nothing left behind, just ashes blowing in the wind

GUY          Good

JASMINE      What?

             *GUY off. HELEN in.*

HELEN     What about your homework

Jasmine

I want you to be happy, that's all

I don't blame you

I blame him

And your father

I know what it's like to be in love

I remember

If we can't live by other people's rules

We'll make our own

We have our values

People will see that, eventually

We'll live as we want

In this house

You will stay here

I know he's buying something

Near the Harbour would be nice

But you'll stay and finish school

Two years, that's all

And do well

That will show them

All these experiences you've been having must be good for something

In academic terms

And meanwhile we'll all get to know each other

Properly

Because after all, there's no rush

You've got all the time in the world

You may find as you grow up

You'll begin to see him differently

Who knows

Someone might come along

Some young man

JASMINE    That doctor's weird

HELEN    I can't send you to Dr Mackay

He knows us

JASMINE    He didn't even talk to me

Just handed them over

HELEN    He was probably embarrassed

It wasn't easy to find him

He does it on principle

He believes they should be freely available even in circumstances like

He's taking a risk

He works for the city council

JASMINE    There were all these marble floors and people in offices

I mean, thanks for finding him but mum

It's the Town Hall

It's a big place to go for just a little pill

HELEN    Darling, I'm sorry

JASMINE    Anyway, they don't work

## Scene 9

*BILL and DAVID.*

DAVID    I've been in Britain

The Lake District

BILL    Was that enjoyable

DAVID     I was at Windscale

BILL    Ah

DAVID    It was human error, not a weakness in the science

Although it could be argued that failing to allow for human error was in fact a weakness in the science

BILL    My daughter's pregnant

DAVID    Yes

What do you want to do

BILL    I thought you might have a suggestion

DAVID    How is she

BILL    I've been sacked

My laboratory's been done away with

I fell foul of someone

DAVID   I can't take on a child

I mean, a baby

I can't explain what happened

I did honestly think I loved her

As soon as I found myself saying it

And of course once you've said it, you want it to be true

I can't marry her, without loving her. You wouldn't want that

What happened wasn't entirely my fault

I know she was only fifteen but she –

No. Forget it

I'll pay for the termination

That goes without saying

I'm not without integrity

I'm trying to tell the truth

I did love her, perhaps, but

When it's gone, it's gone

BILL   You could have

Just not

You could have had the forbearance

Science is selfless

DAVID   You're making me feel like a criminal

Just because I chose a particular profession

Why should I bear the weight of your wishful thinking

BILL        The light's gone out of her

DAVID        Life had been kicking me in the teeth, and suddenly there was this thrill

It's what every man dreams of

BILL        You

So

You have no concept whatever of responsibility

DAVID        Responsibility isn't a concept

It's a feeling

And I don't feel it

BILL        Something I've always believed

Intelligence lifts people up

It has to

Something has to

I admired you

DAVID        You didn't admire me

You admired what you thought reflected your sentimental values

BILL        You're a gentle sort of person, a highly developed human being, you're what people want to evolve to

Becoming like you is supposed to be the remedy to all the

Is this you

Please

If it is, there's nothing

Does nothing make an impression on you

Does nothing strike home

One moment, someone's real to you, they move you, you're fellows, there's a bond

The next, they've vanished from your thoughts as if they'd never existed

As if they'd been something floating in your eye

There has to be a connection from person to person

Doesn't there?

If someone's in pain, you have to feel it, it has to affect you, you have to act on it

Otherwise

There's no such thing as mind, the shared human mind

There's no such thing as the human city, built up brick by brick

In the mind

There's no such thing as culture, or history, nothing is being accumulated, there's no development, no improvement

DAVID   You thought I came with some sort of guarantee

BILL   No growth of fairness, justice, the understanding of how to be good to each other

There's nothing but savagery, for ever

DAVID   There are no guarantees

BILL   There are, if a man's not a reptile

DAVID   I heard something interesting, about bushfires

They've discovered

The trees depend on the fire. The seeds will only germinate if they're burned

A bushfire seems the most terrible thing, the noble forest laid to waste, the suffering of millions of animals

Then they make this extraordinary discovery

The seeds of the trees need the fire

BILL   Why did you pick on her? You couldn't get a proper woman. They'd steer clear of you

DAVID   Did you ask me here to insult me?

BILL   Yeah. Why not

DAVID   I can't marry her, if that's what you want

BILL   It's the last thing I want

DAVID   And yet you actually encouraged our relationship

BILL   Bollocks

DAVID   I've been compromised as well, you know

BILL   What the hell are you talking about?

DAVID   You had it in your power to put an end to the affair. You could have sent me to prison, but you didn't

BILL      As if we'd –

DAVID     You would have been perfectly happy if I'd married her. In my situation, I suppose I was easy prey

BILL      I wouldn't let her marry you if you paid me

DAVID     Paid you? Are you trying to blackmail me?

BILL      What?

DAVID     As a civil servant, I'm vulnerable

Especially to people of your political persuasion

I'm engaged in sensitive work, connected to national security

I warn you

You'll have a difficult time

I'll deny everything

BILL      Get out

DAVID     You'll be the one being accused

BILL      Get out

*DAVID off. HELEN in.*

HELEN     How did it go?

*JASMINE in.*

JASMINE     How did it go?

# Scene 10

*JASMINE, BILL, HELEN.*

JASMINE  You shouldn't have told him

BILL  Why's that

JASMINE  It's putting pressure on him

BILL  You think so

JASMINE  Dad

How can you love someone, then not love them?
That's impossible

Didn't he love me

Then why did he do those things and say those
things

So we're not getting married

BILL  No

HELEN  Jasmine, we have to think about

Your schooling. University. The baby

JASMINE  I'll look after the baby

HELEN  Have you considered adoption

JASMINE  No

HELEN  The other alternative is to look for a doctor

You know what we've always said

Every child a wanted child

JASMINE  I want it

BILL        He says he'll pay for a termination

JASMINE     You asked him!

BILL        No

JASMINE     You did, you asked him

BILL        No

JASMINE     It doesn't matter

HELEN       Jasmine

            If you have this child it will ruin your life. You, in
            return, will ruin its life. You'll be unhappy, the child
            will be unhappy, its children will be unhappy, that
            will be the legacy

JASMINE     Your legacy

            You don't love me

BILL        Of course we do. That's why we

JASMINE     All you care about is your legacy

            My baby will love me

            I won't need anyone

            Not even him

BILL        Jasmine, this is irrational

JASMINE     Don't tell me what's irrational

            I'm surprised you haven't fixed the world. You fix it,
            all right, then you can tell me what to do

            And of course the government's going to listen to
            you on the subject of the forty-hour week

            Just because you know who Khrushchev is

Does he know who you are?

Why don't I go to Mr Menzies and say, 'My dad is very concerned about Australia's endorsement of America's Far East policy'

That will make him sit up

My all-powerful father

You're just a man in a house dreaming you matter somewhere

BILL        I accept that

But

JASMINE        It's my baby

BILL        It's a few cells

JASMINE        How dare you say that about my baby!

BILL        It's his baby too

He doesn't want it

JASMINE        He will when I have it

BILL        Don't be a fool

JASMINE        You don't know anything

BILL        How could you fall for that apology for a man

There's a certain kind of woman that picks the bad apple every time

JASMINE        I didn't even like him!

He's just

Full of himself

Don't tell me I fell for him

You fell for him

I thought you'd be proud of me

BILL    I've always been proud of you

Always

Jasmine

I'm not raising that man's child

# Scene 11

*The house. ROBBO, BILL, GUY.*

ROBBO    And how's baby

BILL    He's a cute little bloke

It remains to be seen who he takes after

ROBBO    Are you coming to film club?

I took the precaution of bringing some insect repellent

BILL    Do you believe in human progress?

ROBBO    Speaking as a member of the Chamber of Commerce, no

Have you heard the latest?

They want to choose an emblem for the shopping centre. Something that typifies the neighbourhood

One wag suggested a slug pellet

But after some discussion, they hit upon the Granny
Smith apple

Which is fair enough

Because Granny Smith dropping a pip into the
ground was a pretty momentous event

Round here

Then they started talking about how to establish this
emblem in the minds of the public

An apple blossom festival was proposed, with floats
and a procession and a contest for Miss Apple
Blossom to be chosen by the Mayor from among the
girl guides

Then the Methodist who runs the pie shop got up
and said it smacked of pagan revelries

Next they proposed a sculpture

Not of Granny Smith

Of an apple

BILL    Everyone believes in human progress. Everyone
distinguishes between different kinds of behaviour,
and that's because they hope to encourage one kind
and discourage another

Everyone thinks they can improve

And there are marks of progress and you fix one and
move towards the next

A piece of knowledge is tested and proved and you
build on it

A certain kind of behaviour is found to be positive
so you learn it, you fix it and it's there. Then you
proceed

Which means there has to be such a thing as
advanced behaviour

I thought if someone chooses a beautiful scientific
life

That would

How could he be in contact with that sort of beauty
and not be shaped by it?

How could it not work on him?

And if it doesn't work, what is there

ROBBO    I said what do we want with a sculpture anyway

We're crying out for a toilet

What's the point of attracting people to the shopping
centre if they're walking round busting for a slash?
No one wants to open their wallet if they're busy
holding on for dear life

Eventually a decision was reached. We're going
to have a toilet with a big green apple on the top.
That'll put us on the map all right

It's *Ivan the Terrible* part two tonight

Something to cheer you up

Film club's been a revelation to me

*Les Quatre Cent Coups*

What a stunner

The way that kid gets pushed to the edge of the sea

BILL     I've got a job

ROBBO    That's good news

BILL     Manufacturing food colourings

ROBBO    Coloured food

         What'll they think of next

BILL     No

         They make the food the colour it's supposed to be

ROBBO    Science never ceases to amaze me

BILL     She used to walk on the playground wall holding my
         hand

         I've never felt so invincible and so able to provide

         She respected me till it happened

         It's because she respected me that it happened

ROBBO    Time we were making tracks

BILL     Robbo, I

ROBBO    I guess you're not in the mood

         My old man had depression

         After he lost his legs

         *ROBBO off.*

BILL     I wish I were dead

         *HELEN in.*

HELEN     Gesell and Ilg

It was our bible, remember?

I must have been insufferable

But when a child's development's at stake

Anyway, you're the one who built her a wooden blast furnace

Jasmine's a wonderful mother

BILL     Just as well, as they've thrown her out of school

HELEN     Bill

There's nothing the matter with you

It's the classic bourgeois malaise

And we're not bourgeois, so cut it out

(*Reads.*) 'Sixteen Weeks…

He awakes to play and he plays to be awake.' Isn't that beautiful?

He's been doing all this for ages

We could try him with mashed banana

Just now in the kitchen he was fascinated by the pressure-cooker, he couldn't take his eyes off the valve going round and round and when a puff of steam came out he laughed, an absolute belly laugh. This tiny little baby with an absolute belly laugh

You're going to have to move all that hi-fi stuff

*HELEN off.*

BILL    (*To GUY.*) I've always lived with her with one eye
on the exit

The exit was always there, so I was able not to leave

The exit consisted of

Some kind of communion with the future of the
world, to which I imagined I was invited

Or even, communion with some like-minded person

But anyway

Some joyful, fortifying continuity, with the horrors of
the past being gradually whittled away

Are they being whittled away? Can they be?

Even now, I still sometimes think

It's just round the corner

We've got the whole social mechanism practically in
our hands

If we could simply make a few minor adjustments

What hands

What adjustments

Wishful thinking

And I used to be able to do it, and now I can't

There's no exit

There's just us

And look at us

*JASMINE in with baby and a basket of washing.*

JASMINE    Dad

> *JASMINE hands the baby to BILL and exits.*

> *End.*